Young Vic in association with Amnesty International

The Container

by Clare Bayley

This production opened on 15 July 2009 at the Young Vic

Mariam   **Amber Agar**
Fatima   **Doreene Blackstock**
Jemal   **Abhin Galeya**
Asha   **Mercy Ojelade**
Ahmed   **Hassani Shapi**
The Agent   **Chris Spyrides**

Direction   **Tom Wright**
Design   **Naomi Dawson**
Sound   **Adrienne Quartly**
Dialect Coach   **Jeffery Daniel**
Fight Direction   **Alison de Burgh**

Stage Manager   **Emily Peake**
Deputy Stage Manager   **Holly Handel**
Costume Supervisor   **Catherine Kodicek**
Costume Assistant   **Cherish Mutambara**

Producer   **Debra Hauer**

With thanks to Phil and Perry at First Containers, the staff of the Wellington Hospital, Kim Handel, Urban Space Management Ltd and Container City, Lambeth Council, Carolyn Brown, Felicity Feeny, Garden Court Chambers, Mr and Mrs James Golob, the Hilden Trust, Laura Devine Solicitors, Jonathan Levy, Alan Rickman, Tony and Nicola Schlesinger, Tom Stoppard, Wesley Gryk Solicitors, Tim Roseman of Theatre503 and Ice and Fire.

The Container was first developed as a collaboration between Creative Partnerships, Thames Gateway and Nimblefish directed by Elgiva Field. It was then premiered at the Edinburgh Fringe Festival directed by Tom Wright in 2007 with the following cast:

Fatima   **Doreene Blackstock**
Jemal   **William El-Gardi**
Mariam   **Deborah Leveroy**
Ahmad   **Omar Mostafa**
Asha   **Mercy Ojelade**
The Agent   **Chris Spyrides**

Amber Agar Mariam

Theatre includes: *The Man of Mode* (National); *Factors Unforeseen* (Orange Tree Theatre); *The Suppliants* (BAC); *Age Sex Location* (Riverside Studios).
Television includes: *Law & Order, Touch of Frost, Green Wing, Murder City, Totally Frank, Broken News, Eastenders.*

Doreene Blackstock Fatima

Theatre includes: *Any Which Way* (Only Connect Theatre); *Noughts & Crosses* (RSC); *The Container* (Edinburgh Fringe Festival); *One Under* (Tricycle Theatre); *25/7* (Talking Birds Theatre Company, Coventry); *I have before me a Remarkable Document given to me by a Young Lady from Rwanda* (Ice & Fire/Finborough Theatre); *The Gift* (Birmingham Rep Studio /Tricycle); *Downfall & The Carver Chair* (Contact, Manchester); *Leave Taking & Girlie Talk* (Belgrade, Coventry); *Rosie & Jim's Big Theatre Adventure* (Ragdoll Theatre Productions/Oxford Playhouse).
Television includes: *Trinity, Wire in the Blood, Holby City, The History of Tom Jones, The Foundling, Common as Muck II, Gimme, Gimme, Gimme.*

Abhin Galeya Jemal

Theatre includes: *The Hot Zone* (BAC); *Ramayana* (National); *Best of Motives* (Tricycle); *East is East* (New Vic Theatre).
Television includes: *Rome, Final Demand, 10 Days to War, Robin Hood, Waking the Dead, Inspector Lynley Mysteries, Judge John Deed, M.I.T, The Bill.*
Film includes: *The Blue Tower, Wimbledon.*

Mercy Ojelade Asha

Theatre includes: *The Walworth Farce* (National/New York); *The Container* (Edinburgh Fringe Festival); *The Lion & The Jewel* (Barbican Pit & Tour); *Eclipse* (Sydney Opera House Studio).
Television includes: *Ørnen/The Eagle, Holby City, Doctors.*
Film includes: *Incendiary, Ezra, Wake up Call.*

Hassani Shapi Ahmed

Theatre includes: *Don Quixote* (Nuffield Theatre); *Waiting Room for Journeying Souls* (Peepul Theatre); *Coups and Calypsos* (Oval Theatre).
Television includes: *Apparitions, Casualty, Wire in the Blood, The Bill, Whistle Blowers.*
Film includes: *Oggi Sposi, Lezioni Di Cioccolato; Land, Gold, Women; K, Star Wars – The Phantom Menace, The World Is Not Enough, Irina P.*

Chris Spyrides The Agent

Theatre includes: *Sketch your Rocks Off* (Broken Dog & Chocolate Ambulance); *Hell is Other People* (Backbone Productions); *Too Loud* (Reduced Circumstances); *Slupianek* (Origen's Scream); *Julius Caesar* (Globe); *The Tempest* (North Haven Community Theatre); *Doctor Faustus, East* (LSC); *Feel the Fangs of Dracula* (Old Red Melodrama Company); *The News Revue* (Canal Café Theatre); *Don Q* (Labyrinth Theatre); *The Boys Next Door* (Two Colour Theatre).
Film includes: *Proper Man, International Wife Shouting, The Grocer.*

Clare Bayley Writer

The Container was first produced in 2007 in Edinburgh, where it won a Fringe First and the Amnesty International Freedom of Expression award. **Other work includes** *The Shift, Blavatsky* (Young Vic); *The Enchantment,* an English version of the play by Victoria Benedictsson (National Theatre, Cottesloe 2007); *At Sea* (Hotbed Festival, Cambridge 2009); *The Woman Who Swallowed a Pin* (Southwark Playhouse, 2000).

Radio includes: *Heathrow* (for the Urban Scrawl series, on theatrevoice.com 2009); *The Secret Place* (BBC Radio 4 2008); *The Bringer of Sweets.* **Future projects:** *Safekeeping,* site specific sequel to *The Container,* in development with Tom Wright and Meeting Ground; *Blue Sky,* for BBC Radio 4; *Making Capital,* originally commissioned by the National Theatre; and *The Playground,* two-part TV drama.

Tom Wright Direction

Tom has been assistant director at the Young Vic (on the C4 Director's Scheme), Bristol Old Vic, West Yorkshire Playhouse and the RSC.
Directing includes: *The Soul of Ch'ien-Nu Leaves Her Body* (Young Vic); *Tempest* (Southwark Playhouse); *The Water Engine* (Theatre 503/Young Vic); *Workplay* (TIS, Madrid); *Small Waves* (The Powerhouse, Nottingham/Methodica, Vancouver); *Ay Carmela!* (York Theatre Royal & tour); *The Good Person of Sichuan* (The Drum, Birmingham); *The Container* (Edingburgh Fringe, winner Fringe First & Amnesty International Award); two short operas in Selfridges' shoe section (The Opera Group). His drama school productions include work at Rose Bruford, Birmingham SA, Guildford SA, Manchester Met, Mountview and Guildhall. He is artistic director of Vivid Dreams and co-director of Meeting Ground. His work is dedicated to his mentor, Daisaku Ikeda.

Author's thanks

My thanks: to producer Sue Lawther at Creative Partnerships, director Elgiva Field and the creative team; also to Lynette Clark and Hemi Yeroham, William El-Gardi and Deborah Leveroy, Greg Klerxx and Sam Holdsworth of Nimblefish; Nick Kent at the Tricycle Theatre, Deborah Bruce and the actors who took part in the development workshop; Tim Barnden, Garry Kelly, Sonal Ghelani and Hamish Arnott; Osman Ahmed. Special thanks to the many people who told me their stories while I was researching the play, especially Karim from Afghanistan and Asha Kin Duale from Somalia.
My gratitude goes to Debra Hauer and David Lan for their unfailing support for this project.
And very special thanks to Felix and Laurie.

Naomi Dawson Design

Trained at Wimbledon School of Art and Kunstacademie, Maastricht.
Previous work includes: *Senora Carrar's Rifles, The Pope's Wedding, Forest of Thorns* (TPR, Young Vic); *King Pelican, Speed Death of the Radiant Child* (Drum Theatre, Plymouth); *Amgen: Broken* (Sherman Cymru); *If That's All There Is* (Lyric); *State of Emergency, Mariana Pineda* (Gate); *…Sisters* (Gate/Headlong); Can any Mother Help Me? (Foursight & tour); *Stallerhof, Richard III, The Cherry Orchard, Summer Begins* (Southwark Playhouse); *Phaedra's Love* (Barbican Pit/Bristol Old Vic); *Different Perspectives* (Contact Theatre); *Market Tales* (Unicorn); *Attempts on Her Life, Widows, Touched* (BAC); *In Blood, Venezuela, Mud, Trash, Headstone* (Arcola); *Pass the Parcel* (Theatre Royal, Stratford); *A Thought in Three Parts* (Burton Taylor).
Film includes: costume design for short film *Love After a Fashion*; set design for *Fragile* by Idris Khan.
She is also part of artists collective SpRoUt recently exhibiting in Galerija SC, Zagreb.

Adrienne Quartly Sound

Sound design highlights: *The Tragedy of Thomas Hobbes* (RSC); *365* (National Theatre of Scotland); *Stockholm* (Frantic Assembly); *Woyzeck* (St Ann's Warehouse/Gate); *Just Between Ourselves, Private Fears in Public Places* (Royal and Derngate, Northampton); *Small Change* (Sherman Theatre); *93.2fm* (Royal Court); *Nostalgia* (Drum Plymouth); *Playing for Time, A Touch Of The Sun* (Salisbury Playhouse); *Hysteria, Inspector Sands, The Enemy of the People, Silver Birch House, Last Waltz Season, Arcola, Tejas Verdes* (Gate); *Mercy Fine* (Clean Break Theatre).
Composer: *Tragedy of Thomas Hobbes* (RSC); *Lighter Than Air* (Circo Ridiculoso, Pleasance Edinburgh '09); *National Alien Office* (Riverside Studios). www.adriennequartly.com

Jeffery Daniel Dialect Coach

Jeffery recently graduated from Central School of Speech and Drama with an MA in Voice Studies. He has been voice tutor on the acting course at Kingston College, Southbank University and Central.

Alison de Burgh Fight Direction

Recent work includes: *Sus* (Young Vic); *The King and I* (Royal Albert Hall); *Tosca* (Richmond Theatre Royal); *Romeo and Juliet* (Globe); *Macbeth, Harper Regan* (National); *Romeo and Juliet* (RSC); *Romeo and Juliet* (Opera North); *The Dumb Waiter* (West End)
Recent film work includes: *The Dark Room, Mine, Othello Little, Ghosts, Four, Promises Promises.*

The Young Vic

We present the widest variety of classics, new plays, forgotten works and music theatre. We tour and co-produce extensively within the UK and internationally.

Our artists
Our shows are created by some of the world's great theatre people alongside the most adventurous of the younger generation. This fusion makes the Young Vic one of the most exciting theatres in the world.

Our audience
...is famously the youngest and most diverse in London. We encourage those who don't think theatre is 'for them' to make it part of their lives. We give 10% of our tickets to schools and neighbours irrespective of box office demand, and keep prices low.

Our partners near at hand
Each year we engage with 10,000 local people – individuals and groups of all kinds including schools and colleges – by exploring theatre on and off stage. From time to time we invite our neighbours to appear on our stage alongside professionals.

Our partners further away
By co-producing with leading theatre, opera, and dance companies from around the world we challenge ourselves and create shows neither partner could achieve alone.

The Young Vic is a company limited by guarantee, registered in England No. 1188209 VAT Registration No. 236 673 348 The Young Vic (registered charity no. 268876) receives public funding from:

Supporting the Young Vic

The Young Vic relies on the generous support of many trusts, companies and individuals to continue our work on and off stage year on year. For their recent support we thank:

Public Funders
Arts Council England
Equalities and Human
Rights Commission
Southwark Council

Corporate Supporters
American Airlines
Bloomberg
Bupa
Cadbury Schweppes
Foundation
De La Rue Charitable Trust
HSBC Bank plc
J.P. Morgan
KPMG Foundation
London Eye
North Square Capital

The Directors Circle

Big Cheeses
HgCapital
Ingenious Media Plc
Land Securities

Hot Shots
Bloomberg
Blue Rubicon
Clifford Chance LLP
Slaughter and May
Symbian
Taylor Wessing LLP

High Fliers
London Communications
Agency

Trust Supporters
The Arimathea Charitable
Trust
City Parochial Foundation
John S Cohen Foundation
Columbia Foundation Fund
of the Capital Community
Foundation
Dorset Foundation
D'Oyly Carte Charitable
Trust
Equitable Charitable Trust
Eranda Foundation
Ernest Cook Trust
Esmée Fairbairn
Foundation
Garrick Charitable Trust
Genesis Foundation
Goethe-Institut
Help a London Child
Henry Smith Charity
Jerwood Charitable
Foundation
John Ellerman Foundation
The Limbourne Trust
Man Group plc Charitable
Trust
Martin Bowley Charitable
Trust
Paul Hamlyn Foundation
Peter Moores Foundation
Pidem Fund
Quercus Charitable Trust
Steel Charitable Trust
The Worshipful Company of
Grocers

Friends of the Young Vic

Production Supporters
Tony & Gisela Bloom
Chris & Jane Lucas
Nadine Majaro &
Roger Pilgrim
Miles Morland
Anda & Bill Winters

Best Friends
Jane Attias
Chris & Frances Bates
Alex & Angela Bernstein
The Bickertons
Katie Bradford
Sarah Hall
Richard Hardman & Family
Nik Holttum & Helen
Brannigan
Suzanne & Michael
Johnson
Tom Keatinge
John Kinder & Gerry
Downey
Tim & Theresa Lloyd
Simon & Midge Palley
Charles & Donna Scott
Justin Shinebourne
Richard & Julie Slater
Jack & Joanne Tracy
Leo & Susan van der
Linden
Rob Wallace
Edgar & Judith Wallner

Great Friends
Angus Aynsley &
Miel de Botton Aynsley
Tim & Caroline Clark
Robyn Durie
Maureen Elton
Jenny Hall
Sheila & John Harvey
Susan Hyland
Tony Mackintosh
Ian McKellen
Frank & Helen Neale
Anthony & Sally Salz
Mr & Mrs Bruce R Snider
Donna & Richard Vinter
Jimmy & Carol Walker

The Container is produced in association with Amnesty International.

Amnesty International

Article 19 of the Universal Declaration of Human Rights: Everyone has the right to freedom of opinion and expression and to seek, receive and impart information and ideas through any media and regardless of frontiers.

Amnesty International is a movement of ordinary people from across the world standing up for humanity and human rights. Our purpose is to protect individuals wherever justice, fairness, freedom and truth are denied.

Amnesty International's arts work is programmed under the Amnesty Arts Fund umbrella which brings human rights issues to a wider audience and encourages creative activism.

www.amnesty.org.uk

The Container education project is co-produced with Meeting Ground Theatre Company.

Meeting Ground was founded in 1984 to give central space to "lost or unacknowledged voices" by creating productions which explore the lives of people ignored or demonised by the media. Previous work includes workshops at the Royal Court with Iraqi and Iranian artists, the *War Stories* project which brought together theatre workers from Gaza, Serbia, Bosnia, Algeria for a theatre project in Rumania, devised piece *Shoes* and new play *Small Waves* dealing with life in exile.

Meeting Ground is currently working with Clare Bayley to create a companion piece to *The Container*, *Safe Keeping*, for production next year. For updates on this, other Meeting Ground projects and director Tom Wright's work please visit: www.tomwrightdirector.com

THE CONTAINER

Clare Bayley

For Chris

Characters

FATIMA, *Somali woman, forties*

ASHA, *Somali woman, fifteen*

JEMAL, *Turkish Kurd, twenties*

AHMAD, *Afghan man, fifties*

MARIAM, *Afghan woman, twenties*

THE AGENT, *Turkish*

The play contains lines in Turkish, Somali and Pashto. As Pashto uses the Arabic script, all lines in Pashto are phonetically transcribed.

Although this play was written to be performed in an actual container, it could also be performed in more conventional venues.

This text went to press before the end of rehearsals and may differ slightly from the play as performed.

Scene One

A container, which appears to be empty except for some pallets. The drone of an engine is heard. As the play begins, the lorry is heard to come to a halt. FATIMA, ASHA, JEMAL *and* AHMAD *emerge from their hiding places behind and under the pallets. They whisper.*

FATIMA. What happened? Have we stopped?

JEMAL. Yes.

AHMAD. Why are we stopping? What is going on?

JEMAL. Keep your voice down.

FATIMA. Someone will let us out.

JEMAL. Shhhh.

AHMAD. What?

JEMAL. I'm listening.

AHMAD. What can you hear?

JEMAL. Nothing, if you don't shut up.

AHMAD. Did you hear something?

JEMAL. Shut up. There could be police outside.

FATIMA. Police? Outside?

JEMAL. Shut up, do you hear me? Shut up.

   Silence.

   FATIMA *stands and starts to move around.*

   What you doing?

   FATIMA *ignores him.*

   What you doing?!

FATIMA. I'm stretching my legs.

JEMAL. Keep still, can't you? You'll make noise.

FATIMA. My leg is dead. I have to move.

JEMAL. Sit down, you stupid woman!

FATIMA. Don't speak like that to me!

AHMAD. Shhhh. Both of you. You want to get us all caught?

FATIMA. He is so rude, this man!

AHMAD. Just sit down.

JEMAL. I'm trying to hear what's going on.

AHMAD. Is it police?

FATIMA. There's no need to be so rude.

A pause.

AHMAD. Can you hear something?

JEMAL *listens.*

JEMAL. Nothing. I can't hear anything.

A pause. JEMAL *gives up and sits down.*

FATIMA. Why have we stopped?

Nobody answers her.

You. Rude man. Why have we stopped?

JEMAL. I'm not the fucking tour guide, am I? I don't fucking know why we've stopped.

FATIMA. Don't listen to him, Asha. You see? Always so rude. And bad language, too.

The doors are opened. The sudden light is dazzling. They all melt back into their hiding places.

MARIAM *enters.*

She stands, trying to see in the darkness, her hand over her mouth and nose, because of the smell in there. She retches. The doors are closed behind her. AHMAD *emerges.*

AHMAD. Where's the agent?

FATIMA. Where is the food?

JEMAL. Do you know where we are?

The truck starts moving.

FATIMA. We are moving again. Where is our food?

JEMAL. Did you see the agent?

AHMAD. Did he give you some food?

FATIMA. Yes – and water. Where is the water?

JEMAL. Do you know where we are?

Do you speak English?

FATIMA. I think she is sick.

MARIAM. I don't know the name. The north of Italy. Very
north.

JEMAL. Near the border?

MARIAM *nods.*

The border with Switzerland?

MARIAM. With France. We will go through France.

JEMAL. Good. That's good. Two, three more days.

MARIAM *sits.*

MARIAM. How long have you been in here?

AHMAD *shrugs.*

AHMAD. Is it three days or four?

JEMAL *nods.*

We came across from Turkey, through the Balkans. We have
no food left, and only a little water.

FATIMA. My daughter is very hungry. Very hungry.

JEMAL. Yeah, you always say it's your daughter who's hungry,
but then you eat all her food yourself, don't you? Eh?

FATIMA. Don't listen to this man. He is a very bad man. Very bad.

AHMAD. How long have you been travelling?

MARIAM. I was in Milan for a month. But I left my country three months ago.

AHMAD. The agent, he's supposed to bring us food, that was the agreement, but he hasn't brought anything.

JEMAL. Where you from, then?

MARIAM. From Afghanistan.

AHMAD (*in Pashto*). *Pa her ram ghlasp*. [Welcome.]

JEMAL. Speak in English.

AHMAD (*in Pashto*). *Hagha khawkh gain chi pam mar sap ho shi*. [He likes to know everything that's going on.]

AHMAD *laughs loudly.*

JEMAL. We're all Europeans now. Speak in English.

AHMAD. You don't like to feel you don't know what's going on, do you? She is from my country.

FATIMA. How many more days, then? Two more days?

AHMAD. Could be more.

FATIMA. We're supposed to stop. He said we would stop. Why didn't he let us out? It stinks in here.

AHMAD. He was supposed to bring us food, too. Did he give you food?

JEMAL. See how friendly he is? He only talks if he wants something.

AHMAD. The agent said he would –

JEMAL. Yes, yes, he said he would bring food, he said he would stop to let us out, he said many things.

FATIMA. He said he will take us to England.

AHMAD. I don't want to starve to death inside this lorry.

JEMAL. Starve! You! (*He laughs*.) Starve!

AHMAD. What?

JEMAL. You don't look as if you're starving.

FATIMA *laughs too*.

FATIMA. He has a good stomach on him.

JEMAL. I can't see it getting any smaller.

AHMAD. Now they're laughing at me. You people. You don't know what I've been through to get here.

JEMAL. We're all the same here.

AHMAD. Oh yes? I don't think we are all the same.

JEMAL. What's that supposed to mean?

AHMAD. We are not all the same. I should not be travelling like this. I am a businessman.

JEMAL. Oh, I see. You're saying you're better than me?

AHMAD. All I'm saying is, we all different.

JEMAL. Yes, we're different. You're fat. I'm thin. We've got no food. But has she? We don't know.

MARIAM. I have only a little food.

AHMAD. You have some?

FATIMA. And water? You have water?

MARIAM. I have water. I have some bread. And chocolate.

FATIMA. My daughter is very hungry.

She gets up.

JEMAL. You going to take her food?

FATIMA. It's for my daughter.

MARIAM *gives her some bread. She offers the rest of the food to the others*.

MARIAM. Please, take it.

JEMAL. What are you going to give her for her chocolate, Mr Fat Man?

AHMAD. It is freely given.

Everyone has some. JEMAL *wraps his up and puts it in his pocket.*

JEMAL. You should save some for later. We don't know when we're going to eat again.

AHMAD. If you're not hungry now, let someone have it who is.

JEMAL (*to* MARIAM). You keep some bread for yourself.

FATIMA. Look at us – it's a shame! So excited for two little bits of bread and some chocolate. But England is a fine place. There is money there. My son says even the street cleaners have mobile phones.

JEMAL *laughs.*

Yes! It's true.

JEMAL. Is that the same son who says he's living in Piccadilly?

FATIMA. Yes. He is waiting for us. He will look after us.

JEMAL. Piccadilly?

JEMAL *laughs again.*

He's doing very well for himself, then, if he's living in Piccadilly.

FATIMA. He has a good job. Good money. He sent money to me to pay agent.

JEMAL. Yeah? What's that, then? Cleaning toilets? Washing windscreens at the traffic lights?

FATIMA. He says London is a fine city. So big! You can drive in a car for three hours and still you are in London. Think of that!

JEMAL. And what does he say about English people, your son?

FATIMA. They are quite civilised.

AHMAD. The English are good businessmen.

ASHA. English people are kind. They welcome people from all over the world.

JEMAL. Everyone lies to his family back home.

FATIMA. He says the Queen is really German. Her husband is a Greek. And the government are all Jews or Scottish. So, you see, they understand.

JEMAL. They understand there's enough foreigners in their country and they don't want any more.

AHMAD. Why do you know so much about England?

JEMAL. Never mind.

FATIMA. He was always my sweetest boy. He always wanted to please his mama. I could have gone to stay with my other son in Holland or my daughter in Belgium. But I said, no! I want to be with my firstborn, my Nuruddin. He wrote to me saying, Mama, you will miss the company of your daughter and in London the weather is very bad. But I say, wherever he is, is where my sun shines.

JEMAL. *Insh'allah*.

FATIMA. What?

MARIAM *almost faints*.

AHMAD (*to* MARIAM). Are you sick?

MARIAM. I am tired.

FATIMA. My sweetest boy. My firstborn.

AHMAD. We don't want sickness in here.

MARIAM. I am OK.

AHMAD. This bloody fighting in our country. Always fighting. I'm not for the Taliban, but at least when they were in power there was not fighting. You could run a business, live a normal life. You have travelled all the way alone?

MARIAM *barely nods, feeling very unwell now*.

FATIMA. All I wanted was to get him safe out of the country. And the others.

AHMAD. All we need is to get on with our business. But there is always fighting. It's not right for a young woman to travel alone. Where is your husband?

MARIAM. My husband is dead.

AHMAD. The fighting, you see? Everyone dead. Women, alone. A widow, at her age. (*To* MARIAM, *in Pashto*.) *Tas oa khom zai vasty? Kabul?* [Where are you from? Kabul?]

What are they going to get at the end of it? No infrastructure. No commerce. No future for our kids.

(*To* MARIAM.) You are tired, you must rest.

She's tired. Just a young girl. You see, people like her and me, we just want to make a life for ourselves.

FATIMA. She is sick. Is she sick?

MARIAM. Where can I . . . ?

AHMAD. She needs to rest.

MARIAM. I need –

She throws up.

AHMAD. Uh! What is this!?

She's sick again.

JEMAL. We have to smell that for days now.

FATIMA. She is sick. I said she was sick.

That's why she didn't want her food.

AHMAD. Clean it up! Clean it up.

MARIAM *slumps down, exhausted.*

FATIMA. You clean it up! You the one so friendly.

ASHA *gets a cloth, pours a little water on it to wipe* MARIAM's *face.*

AHMAD. Hey! We haven't got much drinking water left.

ASHA *tends to* MARIAM.

JEMAL. Here's a plastic bag. In case it happens again.

AHMAD. I can't sit near this stink.

He moves away. ASHA *cleans up the sick.*

FATIMA. Don't touch that! If she's sick, we will all be sick in a few days.

ASHA. Someone has to clean it.

JEMAL. You'd better get used to doing the jobs nobody else wants to do. The dirty jobs. That's what they'll offer you in England.

AHMAD. How much longer will we be in here? I can't stand it. It's so hot I can't breathe!

JEMAL. Then get out. Next time we stop, bang on the side, tell the driver you want to get out.

AHMAD *dismisses* JEMAL *with a gesture.*

A man like you shouldn't be travelling like this. A high-class businessman. You should take the plane. First class.

ASHA. She's resting now.

AHMAD. Lucky for her she can sleep with this stink. She shouldn't be travelling on her own.

FATIMA (*in Somali*). *Kaalay inta gabaryahay. Hataaban ayada, hadii kale waad jiran. Kaalay. Waxaan rabaa inaan ku'caawiyo.* [Come here, girl. Leave her. You will get sick. Come. I need you to help me. Come.]

FATIMA *holds up a piece of cloth, with which* ASHA *will shield her.*

JEMAL. Don't you think it stinks enough in here? Can't you hold on?

FATIMA (*in Somali*). *Kaalay, Asha. Iloow ninkaas.* [Come, Asha. Ignore that man.]

JEMAL *groans, lies down and covers his head with his jacket.* AHMAD *groans too, and lies with his face turned away.* FATIMA *and* ASHA *retreat into a corner, where* ASHA *holds the cloth while her mother squats on the bucket.*

AHMAD. Let me out of here. Please. Let me get out. So many days in here – I can't stand it any more!

Blackout.

Scene Two

As the lights come back up, everyone is asleep except ASHA. *After a moment,* MARIAM *sits up.* ASHA *moves closer to her.*

ASHA. Are you sick?

MARIAM. No. I'm not sick. Thank you. You helped me.

ASHA. I'm not afraid of sickness. In the refugee camp many people were sick. But sick people don't hurt you.

MARIAM. Your mother is afraid of sickness.

ASHA. She is not really my mother. She calls herself my mother. My mother got sick and died.

This one is my auntie.

MARIAM. Why are you travelling with her?

ASHA. There is no one else left. My father never came back. My mother went to get money from the men on the highway. That's why she got sick. My sister, Salma, was going to look after me when my mother died. But when they took her away, only Auntie was left.

I had to come with her.

MARIAM. Where are you going?

ASHA. To England. She is going to see her son. But I have another plan. Where are you going?

MARIAM. I don't know. To somewhere safe.

A beat.

ASHA. You are going to England, too. It is safe in England.

MARIAM *doesn't answer.*

They all complain about this truck. But I like this truck. In this truck we are safe.

MARIAM. For a while.

ASHA. I came across the sea. I came in a boat. Did you come in a boat?

MARIAM. No.

ASHA. I came in a boat. A very small boat with many of us on it. We saw the police boats, but they didn't see us in the darkness. There were men with knives to keep us quiet.

You come from far away, like the fat man. How did you get across the water?

MARIAM. There's no sea. I came by land. By truck. Many trucks.

ASHA. To Italy.

MARIAM. In the end, yes.

ASHA. Where else?

MARIAM. You ask many questions.

ASHA. I'm friendly.

What is your name?

MARIAM. Mariam.

ASHA. Mariam. You came to find someone. Like me.

MARIAM. You are very quiet when your auntie is awake.

ASHA. When she is asleep I find out about people.

You are safe in this truck.

MARIAM *doesn't reply.*

I like you. You are a good person.

You are like my sister. They took my sister away. But they won't take you away.

Why are you going to England?

MARIAM. I told you already.

ASHA. You have a gun in your bag.

I know about everyone in here. Him, over there – (*She points to* AHMAD.) He has a lot of money.

And him – (*She points to* JEMAL.) He has food. But you have a gun.

MARIAM. You looked in my bag when I was asleep?

ASHA. Have you ever used your gun?

MARIAM. No.

ASHA. If I had had a gun, I would have used it. The men who took my sister had guns. If I had one, I would have stopped them.

MARIAM. I wish I had never had to see a gun.

ASHA. They left Salma's baby with me. He cried and cried. I tried to feed him. But no milk would come. I was only a little girl then.

Do you want some chewing gum?

MARIAM. Chewing gum?

ASHA *nods.* MARIAM *takes a piece.*

Thank you.

ASHA. Why are you sick?

MARIAM. I'm not sick.

ASHA. But you were sick.

MARIAM. It's my secret.

ASHA. Tell me.

MARIAM. Secrets are not to be told. You know that.

ASHA. You are my friend. I will tell you my secret.

She starts to rummage in her bag.

MARIAM. No. It is best not to know other people's secrets.

ASHA. Where is it? It must be here.

MARIAM. What is your name?

ASHA. Asha.

MARIAM *takes her by the arm.*

MARIAM. Asha, no. Don't tell your secrets.

ASHA. It is here.

She takes out a letter.

MARIAM. I don't want to know.

ASHA. You have a baby in your belly. That is your secret.

MARIAM. How do you know?

ASHA. I know. My auntie thinks I am stupid but I know some things.

Did your husband know you had a child?

MARIAM *nods.*

Then he will watch over you and keep you safe to London.

A beat.

MARIAM. Don't tell them. I don't want them to know.

ASHA. I promise. But I will tell you my secret. Then it is fair.

I have a letter. See? A letter.

ASHA *produces a letter.*

This letter is for the Queen of England.

MARIAM. The Queen?

JEMAL *stirs, starts to wake.*

ASHA. I know a very important man. He is a king in my country. And he wrote this letter to tell Her Majesty I am a good girl and I work hard and I will make a good servant for her.

MARIAM. Asha!

JEMAL *wakes and listens.*

ASHA. He is a very important man. I think he has met the Queen already. And so I will give her this letter and she will give me a job.

MARIAM. Why do you want to be a servant, little sister? You can be more than a servant.

ASHA. But a servant to a queen . . . !

MARIAM. You must go to school. In England, you can go to school.

ASHA *looks dubious.*

Then you can learn to write your own letters.

ASHA *is unconvinced.*

ASHA. Can you write your own letters?

MARIAM. Of course! I am a teacher.

ASHA. A teacher!

MARIAM. I was a teacher. Before they stopped me.

ASHA. Who stopped you?

MARIAM. It doesn't matter now.

ASHA. Tell me. Then I can learn something.

MARIAM. There are powerful men back there, in my country, who won't let women be teachers. We thought they had gone, but they came back. They punish girls who try to go to school. They kill teachers to stop them teaching girls. That shows you how important it is to learn. In England, no one will stop you.

ASHA. Yes. First I will give this letter to the Queen of England. And she will give me a job. And *then* I will go to school.

JEMAL *starts laughing.*

ASHA *swiftly hides the letter away.*

JEMAL. You're going to be a servant to the Queen of England?

ASHA. I am not talking to you.

   AHMAD *has also woken*.

AHMAD. What?

JEMAL. She says she's going to work for the Queen of England.

MARIAM. Shhhh. Don't laugh at her.

JEMAL. She thinks the Queen's going to give her a job.

   AHMAD *laughs too*.

ASHA. Don't laugh. You don't believe me, but I have it here, see.

JEMAL. What, and this man, the man who wrote your letter, he thinks that the Queen –

MARIAM. Leave her alone. She has a letter. She doesn't want her mother to know.

ASHA. You don't know me. You don't know who I am.

JEMAL. OK. OK! I believe you. The Queen of England.

AHMAD. Why don't you want your mother to know?

ASHA. It's my job. My letter. Don't *laugh* at me.

AHMAD. I won't tease you. Give me some water.

   AHMAD *drinks*. ASHA *puts her letter away*.

JEMAL. Hey! Not so much water.

   FATIMA *starts to stir*.

MARIAM. Shhhh.

AHMAD. I need to drink. I don't feel good. I am very hot.

JEMAL. We're all hot in here.

AHMAD. I hope I am not sick like this woman.

FATIMA. Asha. Have these men been talking to you?

ASHA *shakes her head.*

JEMAL. She doesn't like talking to us. I think she has a secret.

He and AHMAD *laugh.*

FATIMA *is going through her bags.*

FATIMA. Did someone touch these bags when I was sleeping?

ASHA *shakes her head.*

AHMAD. What have you got in there you're so worried about?

FATIMA. Nothing. I have nothing.

JEMAL. There's a lot of nothing there.

FATIMA. If you have rice and water, you can always survive. When I left my house I didn't think about my television or my clothes or my furniture. I just took my gold and then I went to the kitchen and I took rice and sugar and water. In the camp we survived on only rice. For all these years.

JEMAL. Are you going to cook us all some rice in here? Good. Because we're all hungry. So cook us some rice.

FATIMA. If I had a pot –

JEMAL. Yes.

FATIMA. If I could light a fire –

JEMAL. Yes?

FATIMA. If there was water –

JEMAL. Yeah, but there isn't, is there? No pot, no fire, no water. So shut up about your bloody rice.

AHMAD. I was sitting close to her. I think she made me sick.

He goes to the bucket, takes it behind some boxes for privacy.

JEMAL. Some people say the Queen of England doesn't go to the toilet.

FATIMA. What is wrong with this man?

JEMAL. If she doesn't go to the toilet, she must be full of shit.

He laughs.

FATIMA. He is disgusting.

JEMAL. Full of shit.

FATIMA. What about you?

JEMAL. Eh?

FATIMA. Tell us. Come on. Where are you coming from?

JEMAL. Me?

FATIMA. Yes. You. You know so much. Tell us something.

JEMAL. None of your business.

FATIMA. You don't want to tell us? But you always telling us what to do. I know what you not telling us.

JEMAL. Go on.

FATIMA. You speak his language, him out there. You're working with him, aren't you? You're not like us.

JEMAL. Working with the agent?

FATIMA. Yes. That's why you won't tell us.

JEMAL. You've got it wrong.

FATIMA. Why don't you tell us where you've come from?

JEMAL. I speak his language, yes. I speak Turkish. But he's a Turk, and I'm a Kurd. That's the difference. Do you see?

FATIMA. I asked you a question.

JEMAL. In Turkey, Kurds speak Turkish. You know why? They used to put us in prison if we spoke our own language. In Turkey, the prisons are still full of Kurds.

FATIMA. I can tell when I can't trust someone.

JEMAL. He's the one you shouldn't trust. He's an agent. I'm a refugee. That's the difference. You understand? Because that's an important difference. I know about agents. This is the third time I'm trying to get into this fucking country. That's why I know about it. OK. OK?

FATIMA. OK. OK.

The lorry jolts and comes to a halt.

MARIAM. We've stopped.

They wait. AHMAD *comes hurrying back from the bucket, pulling up his trousers.*

FATIMA. Are we at the border? Is this the border now?

AHMAD. He's going to bring us some food at last.

JEMAL. Shhhh.

A silence. They wait, ready to hide if the doors start to open.

MARIAM. The French police have machines that can see inside of lorries. They can see the warmth of your body. They can see your heart beating.

FATIMA. That's not true. How could they?

JEMAL. The British test the air to see if people are breathing inside.

MARIAM. Sometimes they use dogs.

FATIMA. Dogs? I don't like dogs.

JEMAL. Keep quiet.

AHMAD. I told you. It's time to eat.

They wait.

FATIMA. Why doesn't he come?

JEMAL. Maybe the driver has to rest. Maybe to get petrol. Just keep quiet.

FATIMA. They must bring us some food!

MARIAM. I can hear voices.

She has her ear to the side of the truck. JEMAL *comes over and listens too.*

FATIMA. Something is wrong. What's going on?

JEMAL. Shhhh!

They wait.

MARIAM. I heard of some people. They were in the back of a lorry. They couldn't get out. Someone took the front off the lorry and left the back behind and forgot about them.

JEMAL. Shut up, can't you? Shut up. It's nothing. It's nothing. You'd rather be in here than back where you were, wouldn't you? Wouldn't you?

Silence.

AHMAD. We don't know where we are. We could be anywhere. We could be on a boat heading for Africa. We don't know.

FATIMA. They say when you are in the bottom of a big ship, then you can't hear nothing. For days and days you hear nothing.

JEMAL. Don't be stupid. When she got on we were where we should be.

MARIAM. It was like this before. There were twelve of us in the back of a truck and we stopped for a long time and suddenly they came in with dogs and chased us out into the woods.

JEMAL. Don't think about it. We are going to get to England. OK?

MARIAM. I don't want to go back to Milan.

I escaped from those men but if I go back there they will find me. They will make me – [work for them.]

JEMAL. Listen! Someone is coming now. Someone is coming in. Hide!

They hide. The AGENT *enters, holding a cloth to his nose because of the smell and carrying carrier bags containing bottles of water. He is agitated. When they see him, they come out from hiding and take the bottles he's handing out.*

AGENT. They call me evil. You know that? They call me evil because I want to help people. You people!

AHMAD. Is this all! Where is the food? We need food to eat!

AGENT. I help people like you who are being tortured in
prisons, people whose houses are being burned, people
whose children are being shot in front of their eyes, people
who have nowhere to live and nothing to eat and who
would be killed if they stayed behind. All these things
happen every day. It's always the same story. I know,
believe me. I hear these stories from the ones who live it.
I help people from all over the world, the same story. And
they say I am evil.

Do you think I'm evil? Eh?

I'm on your side. You know that.

Drink. It's fresh water. Drink.

JEMAL. Is there a problem?

AGENT. Is there a problem? A problem? Yes, there's a
problem. The problem is the governments who don't want
to help people like you. That's who I've got a problem with.
They try every way to keep you people out of their countries.
So, if you take a plane, they fine the airline. You take a
boat, they fine the company. You get in a truck, they fine the
driver. I try every way, every way I can think of, to get you
in. It's like a game. They shut this door – I go round the
side. They stop me. I climb over. They stop me going over.
No problem. I go underneath. You see what I mean? I get
pleasure every time one truckful of you people gets in,
because then I know I fucked them over one more time.

FATIMA. Why have you brought nothing for us to eat?

AGENT. And it costs, of course it costs. Because some people
want to try to exploit the situation, do you understand?
Because they know our weakness. We have plenty of
weakness, and money is our only strength. It's not
businesslike, what these people do. They want to take the
money but they don't want to fulfil their contract. You see?
And they say *I'm* evil.

JEMAL. Who? Who are these people?

AGENT. Everyone. Everyone is trying to take your money and fuck you over. I'm the one who is trying to help you and fuck those bastards over.

AHMAD. So help us then. Food and water, you said. We've paid. Where's the food?

AGENT. Don't worry about the food. Your problem is not the food. If we get moving again I will bring food.

A beat.

JEMAL. What do you mean?

AGENT. I'm the middle man, you know. I risk my own life helping you. What do you think they'll do if they catch me? They put all the blame on us to distract from who's really to blame. The more people get through, the more mad they get. So they lean on the drivers. And the drivers take advantage.

AHMAD. Are you saying there's a problem with the driver?

MARIAM. He's going to make us get out? Is he going to make us get out?

AGENT. Stay calm, OK. We're going to sort this out, OK?

JEMAL (*in Turkish*). *Şoför sorun mu çikariyor?* [Is there a problem with the driver?]

AGENT (*in Turkish*). *Daha fazla para istiyor.* [Yes. He won't go any further unless you all pay him again.]

JEMAL *sits, head in hands, cursing silently.*

MARIAM. He won't take us?

JEMAL (*in Turkish*). *Ne kadar?* [How much does he want?]

AGENT (*in English*). Fifty dollars each.

Everyone understands.

FATIMA. No no no no no. We paid you. We paid you what you asked. So.

AHMAD. Ten thousand dollars I paid!

AGENT. He won't go no further without more money. He says
it costs him nothing to go to the police now. But if he's
caught, with you inside his truck, big fines for him, prison,
maybe. So he wants fifty dollars. Each.

FATIMA. We already paid. This driver, you hired him, you pay
him.

AGENT. I'm on your side. I said that already. I'm helping you.
But it costs me, every kilometre of the road, it costs me. It's
dangerous. It's getting more dangerous. So it's getting more
expensive. This man, this driver, he knows he has the
power. What does he care if the French police lock you all
up? Eh? Me, I care. I care because I don't like to lose my
game. And I care because I care. OK? But I can't pay for
you.

A silence.

Come on. I know you people. You all got money for your
new life. And your new life is so close now. One day and
your new life begins. There, in England, you will be safe. If
you need a house, you will get it. If you need food, you will
get it. If you need a doctor, you can get it.

So close now. One day away. Fifty dollars to wake up with
English sun on your faces.

A pause. AHMAD *fumbles around in a money belt and
silently hands* the AGENT *a wad of notes.*

Good. That's good.

JEMAL. Give it to him when we get there. What's going to
stop him calling the police anyway, if he has our money?

AGENT. No no. He won't, trust me.

JEMAL. We did.

AGENT. Trust me! What other choice do you have?

FATIMA. I don't have any money. I have been in a refugee
camp so many years. Now this is all I have. You can take it.
Take it. I have no money.

She tries to give him the rice and sugar.

AGENT. All you people learn to lie. Of course! You must lie, always, to save your lives. You must lie some more when you get to Dover – I'll tell you what to say. But I know you have money. You have money. Don't you?

FATIMA. We already paid you!

AGENT. You don't want to pay? You don't want to get to London? Then you get out here. No problem. Get out.

JEMAL. I have to get to England.

AGENT. Then it's worth fifty dollars to you.

JEMAL. Tell him we all give twenty dollars.

AGENT. You crazy? He already asked for one hundred, and I told him fifty. That's his last offer. Come on. Where's your money?

JEMAL. OK, OK. Leave it with me. I will get the money from everyone. OK? You come back, I will have the money.

AGENT. It's the same to me if you get it all or you don't. Who pays stays on the truck. You don't pay, you get out here.

JEMAL. I'll get the money.

AGENT. Be quick, eh? We got to keep moving. The driver can't be late. We very close now, you people. Don't be stupid, because we very close now.

He leaves.

JEMAL *rummages in his shoe and gets his money out.*

JEMAL. OK. We need to get this money now. Come on. Don't fuck around. This is serious now. If anyone doesn't pay, we are all in danger. Him, Mr First-Class Businessman, he's paid. I've paid. I know you don't want him to know where you keep your money. I understand. But he's gone now. You pay up.

AHMAD. Why should they trust you? They should pay him themselves, like me.

JEMAL. Yes yes, they'll pay when they see we're all paying. They don't want to be the ones getting out of the lorry.

FATIMA *and* ASHA *are whispering.*

We're heading for the ferry – don't you see? That's why we've got to be quick.

Come on. Put your money in. If anyone gets out we're all in danger.

AHMAD. Why are you taking all the money? Eh? You give me the money and I'll take it to him.

JEMAL. You've paid. You don't need to worry.

AHMAD. No no no. I know your trick. How much did you put in, eh? Let's see.

JEMAL. I'm not tricking. I'm saving time.

AHMAD. Then you'll say someone hasn't put enough in. I see your trick.

JEMAL. Don't waste time. I speak his language. Please!

ASHA *approaches* JEMAL *holding out some notes and a battered old watch.*

ASHA. My mother has only enough for one.

I have this watch. It's worth a hundred dollars. Please, take it.

JEMAL *inspects the watch and hands it to* AHMAD.

JEMAL. This? This isn't worth even two dollars. This isn't enough.

ASHA. It's all I have. Please, sir.

AHMAD *shakes his head and hands the watch back to her.*

JEMAL. Ask your mother again. She's the one who doesn't like you talking to me. How come she won't tell me herself? She's gone quiet now, hasn't she?

ASHA. Take the watch. Please, sir.

JEMAL. It's not enough. Don't look at me like that. It's the agent who's going to throw you off.

ASHA. This is all I have.

JEMAL. Then ask your mother. We all know she's got more in those bags than some old rice.

FATIMA. I have nothing, except what I give to you.

AHMAD. What about your gold? Eh? What happened to all that? You're a cunning woman, you wouldn't let that get lost.

FATIMA. I swear by Allah, my last piece of gold I had to give away to get me and this child across the sea. It was my grandfather's ring, it was very precious to me, it was heavy, worth a lot of money. My mother gave it to my husband, and when he was killed I got it off his dead finger and I said, I will not rest until this ring is on the finger of my first-born son. I kept it all this time until we had to cross the sea and it was my last piece of gold . . .

She breaks down. A pause.

JEMAL. You have enough for either you or your daughter, then. Which one is going to get off the truck?

ASHA (*to* AHMAD). Please, sir, pay for me. I know you have more money there. I am not asking for a gift. I will pay you the money in England. I will pay you the money back.

AHMAD. When you're living in Buckingham Palace?

ASHA. Yes, sir.

FATIMA. She is a good girl. She is simple, but she will do her best. She will keep her word. I know you are a good man underneath. You would not put a young girl in danger.

JEMAL. I'm not putting her in danger! You're her mother! You pay for her.

FATIMA. I have nothing! You search my bags!

She starts to undo her bundles, revealing only rice, sugar and bundles of cloth.

I wanted to bring something to Nuruddin. I understand his letters. He says he is doing so well, so why does he have no proper address? Why do I send letters to a community centre? I wanted to help him, but now I am just an old woman with a few bags of rice, nothing but a burden to him . . .

ASHA. In the name of my dead sister, I beg you, sir, I beg you to help me.

JEMAL. I can put some of it in, but I can't do it all.

(*To* AHMAD.) Come on! We both put some in.

I can't pay it all. Come on! My girlfriend is in England. My baby's in England.

I have to get back to them.

I swore I would get back to them.

ASHA. I will repay you, sir. When we are in England.

JEMAL. If we get to England.

Listen! I have to get back there.

Here – take it.

Your mother should be ashamed of herself.

He gives her the fifty dollars.

ASHA. I thank you, sir. I thank you. You are a good man, sir.

JEMAL (*to* MARIAM). So it's just you now.

He holds out his hat to MARIAM. *She doesn't move.*

Fifty dollars.

MARIAM *shakes her head.* ASHA *and* FATIMA *turn to watch.*

Here we go.

MARIAM *holds out a few coins.*

MARIAM. I have come so far. It costs so much. Twice I was turned back. But he said one short journey and you are in England. So I gave him my last money.

JEMAL. Come on. What's in your bag? Where did you hide the money?

MARIAM. This is all I have.

FATIMA. What else do you have, girl? A watch? A bracelet?

MARIAM *shakes her head.*

MARIAM. I'm sorry.

ASHA. Don't you have a ring or a gold coin your mother
sewed into your clothes?

MARIAM. When I paid the agent I had five euros left. So
I bought the water, some bread and some chocolate for the
journey.

ASHA. The food we ate?

MARIAM *nods.*

A silence.

(*To* AHMAD.) Sir, you are a man from her country. You
are a rich man, and she has nothing. You can pay for her,
sir. Please.

FATIMA. You heard when the man said if one person gets out
here, we are all in danger.

AHMAD. Why are we in danger? One person can get down
and the rest of us carry on.

FATIMA. If someone sees . . .

AHMAD. If he wants to pay for other people, that's his idea.
I can't pay for someone else.

ASHA. But you are rich.

AHMAD. Why has she left her family? Her father? This girl is
sick. Maybe it's best she gets out now. Wait a little, rest,
and carry on her journey when she is well again.

JEMAL. Rest – where? Wait – where?

How is she going to carry on her journey with no money?

AHMAD. If she goes to the authorities, they will give her
treatment.

MARIAM. I'm not sick.

AHMAD. Listen to that – 'I'm not sick.'

We know you're sick. It still stinks in here because you're sick.

ASHA. She's not sick.

MARIAM. Asha!

AHMAD. She's going to make us all sick.

JEMAL. Someone has to pay or she has to get out.

AHMAD. Then you pay for her! You're the one who's so busy telling the rest of us what to do. You pay for her.

JEMAL. I've already paid twice! You pay for her! You fucking pay for her!

JEMAL *attacks* AHMAD. MARIAM *restrains him, and* AHMAD *gets out of the way.*

MARIAM. No! No fighting.

AHMAD. You must have something to sell. You must have something.

MARIAM. I have this.

MARIAM *produces her gun from her bag.*

AHMAD *cowers behind the pallets.* MARIAM *notices his reaction. She briefly wonders whether to play the situation to her advantage.*

A gun is worth a lot of money.

MARIAM *hands the gun to* JEMAL, *who takes it and examines it.*

AHMAD (*blustering*). How did she come to have a gun? What kind of country is it when young girls carry guns!

MARIAM. It was my father's. He fought with the Mujaheddin. But now he has nothing. He gave it to me when they killed my husband.

AHMAD. Who killed your husband? The Americans?

MARIAM. Taliban killed my husband.

AHMAD. Taliban?

MARIAM. He was a teacher. That was his crime. He was a teacher, and he taught girls. When they came back, they killed him. In front of his class. That was to show everyone they will not tolerate teachers for girls.

So then I taught them, secretly. Until they sent me the letter in the night.

That's why I didn't stay in my country.

JEMAL. Is it loaded?

MARIAM. No.

ASHA. A gun is always worth a lot of money.

JEMAL. Not this one!

FATIMA. She is young. She is alone. Take the gun, and argue for her. If he says no, tell him to spare the young girl. Tell him to have pity. He has many dollars already. Tell him.

JEMAL. I'll try. OK? That's all I can do.

AHMAD. Why should she get through and the rest of us have to pay?

MARIAM. At least try for me. Please.

JEMAL. Yes. OK.

JEMAL *bangs on the side*.

The AGENT *comes into the container.*

JEMAL (*in Turkish*). *Bu kiz hariç herkesten parayi topladik. Para yerine bu silahi verse?* [We've got the money from all except this girl. She's got this, she wants to barter.]

The AGENT *looks at* MARIAM'*s gun and shakes his head.*

AGENT. It's not up to me. The driver decides.

ASHA. A gun is worth a lot of money.

AGENT. It's old. It's broken.

You have to pay.

MARIAM. I have only this to pay with.

AGENT. Then get out here.

MARIAM. I paid you to go to England.

AGENT. What's the difference?

MARIAM. I speak English. I speak no French.

AGENT. Then you have to find a way to pay!

> MARIAM *can't pay.*

> You are refugee woman, you know how to pay.

> MARIAM *says nothing.*

> Listen! I'm trying to help you! You have no money, you
> have to do something!

MARIAM. No.

AGENT. We are waiting for you, all these people who want
to get to England. You are lucky, you know, because you're
a woman. What if a man didn't have enough money? Eh?
Then he'd have to just get out of the truck here. You don't
want to get out here, do you? So come on.

MARIAM. I don't want to.

AGENT. Come, come! This truck going to leave soon. You pay
or you get off.

> *He takes her roughly by the arm.*

JEMAL. Leave her alone.

AGENT. You going to pay for her, then? You can't wait. That
driver, he'll call the police.

MARIAM. I don't know what to do.

JEMAL. I don't have the money.

> *Nobody moves.*

ASHA. She's having a baby.

JEMAL. What!

> *The* AGENT *looks at her.*

AGENT. It doesn't show. He won't know.

MARIAM. I am ashamed I have to ask this, but please. If anyone has any money left, if you can put each one a little bit in – one day, I will repay you all. Please.

FATIMA (*to* AHMAD). We know you are a rich man. You too have daughters. If your daughter was in her shoes, you would pray for someone to help her.

AHMAD. No.

ASHA. Your good deeds will be rewarded.

MARIAM (*in Pashto*). *Lutfan zahtah sitam sawal kawam.* [Please. I beg you.]

AHMAD. I have my own children to think of! If I give all my money away, there will be none left for my own children! What kind of father does that?

ASHA. Then who else? Who will give her some money?

MARIAM. Please. I beg you.

FATIMA. She is with child! Who will help her?

Nobody moves.

ASHA. Give her the ring, Auntie.

FATIMA (*in Somali*). *Yaahuu! Maxaad ka hadlaysaa? Mahayo faraanti!* [Shush! What ring? I have no ring!]

ASHA. Give her the ring!

FATIMA (*in Somali*). *Armush.* [Keep your tongue, girl.]

(*In English*.) You know I gave the ring away so you could get across the water.

ASHA *starts tearing at* FATIMA's *hem.*

ASHA. You can't let her go out alone! She has a baby in her belly! What will happen to her?

AHMAD. The authorities will –

ASHA. We know what will happen!

FATIMA (*in Somali*). *Is dajji, Asha*. [Calm down, Asha.] This is France. This is Europe. Nothing bad will happen to her!

AHMAD. They will look after her.

ASHA *looks at* AHMAD.

ASHA. We ate her food.

FATIMA (*in Somali*). *Wajirto waxaan kaqaban karno*. [There is nothing we can do.]

ASHA *goes back to searching in* FATIMA'*s hem*.

ASHA. You give her the ring! I know you have the ring sewn here, in your clothes –

FATIMA. You are getting sick again. (*In Somali*.) *Mahayo faraantigii. Waan gaday*. [I don't have the ring. I sold it.] I sold it. If I still had it, I would have given it for you, eh? Wouldn't I? But I didn't have it for you and I didn't have it for her.

(*In Somali*.) *Mahayo faraantigii*. [I don't have the ring.]

This man paid for you, and he is a good man, and you are a lucky girl, but someone will be kind for her, too, and she will be lucky, too.

Silence. The AGENT *stands up*. MARIAM *gives him the gun*.

MARIAM. Try. At least try. Maybe the driver will be able to sell it.

JEMAL (*in Turkish*). *Aci biraz şu kiza, yaa*. [Have some pity for the young girl.]

MARIAM. Maybe the driver doesn't know about guns. Maybe he doesn't know it's broken.

The AGENT *turns to* MARIAM.

AGENT. Come with me. You ask him yourself.

ASHA. No!

MARIAM. I can't speak any French. I only speak English.

ASHA. She mustn't go!

FATIMA. Shhhh.

AGENT. I translate. It's better if you ask him. It's easy for him to say no to me. To you, it is harder.

ASHA. It isn't safe for her. I know what they do.

JEMAL. Is it safe for her?

AGENT. Yes. No police outside.

FATIMA. But for her, is it safe for her?

AGENT. Yes. It's safe. It's safe.

ASHA. Don't take her away! Don't let them take her! I know who she is!

    MARIAM *goes to* ASHA.

MARIAM. It is better for me to ask for myself.

    ASHA *is very agitated and upset.*

ASHA. No no no.

FATIMA (*in Somali*). *Aah – haka baqin. Way soo noqon.* [Hush – don't worry. She will come back.]

AGENT. Come.

ASHA. They'll take her away! She'll never come back.

FATIMA. This is not Salma, child. This is a different person.

    The AGENT *and* MARIAM *exit.*

    ASHA *is agitated.* FATIMA *is trying to calm and restrain her.*

ASHA. I know what her secret is. I know who she is. You can't see it, but I know.

FATIMA (*in Somali*). *Armush.* [Hush, child.]

ASHA. I know who she is. They took her away. I saw them take her away.

FATIMA (*in Somali*). *Taasi maahan Salma. Tani waa qof kaduwan.* [That is not Salma. That is a different person.]

ASHA. You can't see it is Salma, but the spirits have showed me.

FATIMA. There are no spirits.

ASHA. The spirits are my friends, they are telling me, 'Don't let them take her away again!'

FATIMA. Asha! Listen to me! Asha! (*In Somali.*) *Asha, Idhagayso!* [Asha, listen to me!] There are no spirits. The spirits don't exist.

ASHA. Salma said –

FATIMA. There are no spirits.

With Salma and the soldiers, that was a long time ago. Now is now. You are here with me.

ASHA. You let them take her! You let them! You let them! You could have –

FATIMA *slaps* ASHA.

FATIMA (*in Somali*). *Jooji!* [Stop it!]

JEMAL. Hey! What's going on?

FATIMA. She's confused.

JEMAL. Yeah, but –

FATIMA. She gets confused. She's seen some bad things and she gets mixed up.

ASHA. I saw them take her away.

FATIMA. Yes. But she will be safe. She will come back in a minute.

AHMAD. Is she a bit . . . in the head?

FATIMA. You see what I have to put up with! When I found her she was mad! Crazy-mad! What could I do? I have to look after her. What am I going to do?

ASHA. Why did you keep me if you hate me?

FATIMA. I took you in from the kindness of my heart.

ASHA. You kept me because you were afraid and you wanted a servant to look after you.

FATIMA. What are you talking about, girl?

Have you no gratitude?

ASHA. Gratitude? You treat me as a servant. And Nuruddin was even worse.

FATIMA. You see what I have to put up with? She is a nasty liar.

He was kind to you! He even gave you a chicken.

ASHA. He gave me a chicken. To keep me quiet. So I wouldn't tell the things he did. Why you think he gave me it?

FATIMA (*in Somali*). *Waxaad tahay gabar qalbi xun oo been ii sheegtay.* [You are a wicked girl to tell these lies.]

After all my kindness to you.

Can't you see the girl is crazy-talking?

And now where am I taking you?

ASHA. Where are you taking me?

FATIMA. To England. To safety. I am risking my own life to take you with me.

ASHA. In England they will take us and lock us up and they will call us bad names and do bad things to us which will hurt and they will tell us we are bad and never let us out.

FATIMA. Tell her!

JEMAL. We're going to England. You will be safe there.

ASHA. In England?

JEMAL. In London. Remember. You have friends in high places.

ASHA. London.

JEMAL. Do you still have your letter?

FATIMA. What letter?

JEMAL. You will get a job and get money.

He gets an apple out of his bag and starts to cut it up.

Maybe you will go to school.

AHMAD. Hey, you got food?

ASHA. I'll get a job and get money and send money back, and
my sister will get well again and the baby will stop crying.

FATIMA. She is going to make me crazy, too.

JEMAL. You'll get a new life in England.

FATIMA. Ay ay ay.

ASHA. I've got my letter. I'm going to get a job.

JEMAL. Yes. You are.

ASHA. Am I?

JEMAL. Yes. You are.

FATIMA. OK. Now rest.

JEMAL. Do you like apples?

He gives ASHA *half the apple. She eats it.*

FATIMA *lies down to sleep.* ASHA *looks towards where*
MARIAM *went out.*

ASHA. She won't come back.

JEMAL. Your sister?

ASHA. We will never see her again.

JEMAL. She's at peace.

ASHA *looks at him. She lies down.* JEMAL *finds a cloth
and covers her. Then he goes to listen, to see if he can hear
what's happening to* MARIAM *outside.*

AHMAD. Can you hear anything?

No answer. JEMAL *listens. He strains to hear. We hear
shouting.* MARIAM *cries out. More shouting.*

Don't listen.

JEMAL. Shhhh!

After a moment, JEMAL *can't bear it any longer. He starts to bang on the side of the container.* AHMAD *quickly restrains him, wrestles him to the floor.*

AHMAD. You need to get to England, don't you? What's more important to you?

JEMAL. I can't just do nothing while she –

AHMAD. What's more important to you?

AHMAD *frees* JEMAL.

You're a good man. You tried. What can you do?

But now you need to get to England.

JEMAL *doesn't move. He sits with his head in his hands.*

Blackout.

Scene Three

Lights up. The AGENT *is with them. They are eating bread and something in tins he has brought for them.*

AGENT. The next time we stop, the door will be opened. Then you are in England.

ASHA. Are we going in a boat?

AGENT. No. In the Eurotunnel. Under the sea.

ASHA. Under the sea?

JEMAL. Where will he drop us? By the terminus?

AGENT. Yes, by the terminus, or on the road to London. I don't know.

JEMAL. Where will you be?

AGENT. I put you on the Eurotunnel. Then I go.

FATIMA. But we can't trust this man, this driver!

AGENT. When you are on the Eurotunnel, you are shut in
a metal cage and no one can get in or out, so you are safe.

FATIMA. I don't like this.

AGENT. Trust me. Trust me. Eurotunnel is safe. They don't
search and they don't spray on Eurotunnel.

AHMAD. What do you mean, spray?

AGENT. Eurotunnel is fast and safe. Believe me. I have a
good reputation.

So. He opens the back. And then you are in England. You
all get out, and you split up. Understand? You don't all go
together.

If you are going to claim political asylum, first person you
see, you say you are a refugee.

AHMAD. I'm not a refugee! I'm a businessman!

AGENT. You want to run a business?

You got one million pounds?

You haven't? No?

Then you're illegal immigrant. That's their rules. So if
you're illegal immigrant, you get out of truck, and you hide.

If they catch you, they will ask you lot of questions. Who
brought you, how you come, where you stop along the way
. . . Now. Why they need to know that?

Think.

Why they want to know all that?

So they can stop more people like you getting here. You
going to make it more difficult for people like you? No. So.
You don't tell them nothing. You can't remember. Ten days
ago, you were at home. Now, you are here. That's all you
know. Non-stop travel. Is that true?

So. You know my name?

No.

You know what I look like?

No. Because now I'm gone, and you never saw me in the first place.

ASHA. What if they come in looking and we are not in England yet?

AGENT. This is why you paid me. No one will come in looking before England. OK. I go now.

ASHA *stops him.*

ASHA. Where is Mariam? Please, sir, can you tell me what happened to her?

AGENT. Don't worry about her now. You going to get your new life now.

He exits.

AHMAD. I don't trust that man, but I wish he was coming with us all the way. What's happening out there? Are we on the train already?

JEMAL. It's time to get our stories straight, now. He's right, it's very important. What we say makes a big difference.

FATIMA. You stop telling us what we got to do! You just the same as us, so you say. So you don't tell us what to do.

JEMAL. No. I'm not the same as you. You haven't spent three months living in a cardboard box in Calais, outside the terminus. I have. There are hundreds of people like us out there, living rough, hiding from the police. Every night they try and get on a train or a truck to get across the sea. That was me. I'm not going back to that again.

ASHA. You were here already?

JEMAL. We must lie. But it must be good lying. Clever lying. Not stupid lying.

ASHA. I don't understand. You lived in England. Why can't you go back?

JEMAL. They turned down my application. After all those years, living in England, going to school there, then they said go back to Turkey. Turkey is safe now for Kurds. Turkey is almost Europe now.

A few months after they sent me back, they changed the law. If it had been a few months later, I could be a British citizen now. If my girlfriend was British then I'd have a chance. But she isn't.

ASHA. Why don't you tell the British that your baby is there? They are kind people. They will allow you.

JEMAL. My baby was born when I was in detention. They didn't care.

They don't want us in their country! It doesn't matter what our story is. They use the law to trick us.

I failed before. But this time I'm going to get back into that country any way I can. I know how to, you see?

I'm going to say I'm from Iraq. I've come all the way from Baghdad, non-stop travel. Clever lying, you see.

I'll keep trying until I get there.

FATIMA. I'm not going back. Where are they going to send me? There's no government there. Only war. They can't send me back to the camp.

JEMAL. That's why they want to know how we got here. If you tell them the truck stopped in Italy, they'll send you back to Italy.

ASHA. We can't go back. I don't want to go back!

JEMAL. Have you still got your letter? Keep hold of your letter.

FATIMA. What is this letter?

JEMAL. Don't worry. We will be OK.

Think how strong we have been, just to get here! And now we have to be clever.

AHMAD. It's the same in everything in life. The clever ones succeed, the others fail.

ASHA. People will always trick and lie and fight. That's why we are here.

JEMAL. Some people are good. Some people are bad. But governments are bad in any place you go to.

The truck stops again. A few jolts.

JEMAL. Shhhh. Maybe they're putting us in the train now. Keep quiet.

ASHA. How long is the tunnel?

JEMAL. It takes about forty minutes.

ASHA. Forty minutes and then we are in England?

JEMAL. Forty minutes. You'd better get smartened up for your job interview.

ASHA. You don't believe me that I'm going to meet the Queen.

The container jolts some more. They wait.

AHMAD. We must be on the train now. Do you think we're on the train?

They wait. Silence.

FATIMA. I think we are on the train now. Soon we will be in England.

Silence.

ASHA. I can't feel us moving.

FATIMA. Soon our journey will be over.

AHMAD. Are we moving?

ASHA. Are we there?

Do you think we have arrived?

Nobody answers.

Slow fade.

The End.

A Nick Hern Book

The Container first published in Great Britain in 2007 as a paperback original by Nick Hern Books Limited, The Glasshouse, 49a Goldhawk Road, London W12 8QP

Reprinted in this revised edition in 2009 in association with the Young Vic Theatre, London

Reprinted 2013

The Container copyright © 2007, 2009 Clare Bayley

Clare Bayley has asserted her moral right to be identified as the author of this work

Cover image designed by Intro (www.introwebsite.com)

Typeset by Country Setting, Kingsdown, Kent CT14 8ES
Printed and bound in Great Britain by Mimeo Ltd, Huntingdon, Cambridgeshire PE29 6XX

A CIP catalogue record for this book is available from the British Library

ISBN 978 1 84842 073 1

CAUTION All rights whatsoever in this play are strictly reserved. Requests to reproduce the text in whole or in part should be addressed to the publisher.

Amateur Performing Rights Applications for performance, including readings and excerpts, by amateurs in the English language throughout the world should be addressed to the Performing Rights Manager, Nick Hern Books, The Glasshouse, 49a Goldhawk Road, London W12 8QP, *tel* +44 (0)20 8749 4953, *e-mail* info@nickhernbooks.co.uk, except as follows:

Australia: ORiGiN Theatrical, Level 1, 213 Clarence Street, Sydney NSW 2000, tel +61 (2) 8514 5201, email enquiries@originmusic.com.au, web www.origintheatrical.com.au

New Zealand: Play Bureau, PO Box 9013, St Clair, Dunedin 9047, *tel* (3) 455 9959, *e-mail* play.bureau.nz@xtra.co.nz

United States of America and Canada: United Agents, see details below.

Professional Performing Rights Application for performance by professionals in any medium and in any language throughout the world (and for amateur and stock rights in USA and Canada) should be addressed to United Agents, 12–26 Lexington Street, London W1F 0LE, *tel* +44 (0)20 3214 0800, *fax* +44 (0)20 3214 0801, *e-mail* info@unitedagents.co.uk

No performance of any kind may be given unless a licence has been obtained. Applications should be made before rehearsals begin. Publication of this play does not necessarily indicate its availability for amateur performance.

Woodland
CARBON
www.woodlandcarbon.co.uk
NICK HERN BOOKS
Printed on Carbon Captured paper